Copyright © 2021 by Eboni Sawyer
All rights reserved. No part of this book may be reproduced or used in any manner without written permission of the copyright owner except in the case of reprints in a book review.

First hardcover edition, April 2021
Design by Mykel L. Brooks
Printed in the United States

ISBN: 9781734828528

Published in the United States by Evolving Still Publishing
a division of Evolving Still, LLC
Detroit, MI
www.evolvingstill.com

Evolving Still Publishing books are available at special discounts for bulk purchases for sales promotions or corporate use. Special editions, including personalized covers, excerpts of existing books or books with corporate logos, can be created in large quantities for special needs. For more information, contact Evolving Still Publishing at contact@evolvingstill.com.

Letter From the Author

When I first started Evolving Still, I had no idea how many people it would reach but to my surprise we keep growing and growing. We have officially been on this journey of evolving for one full year. If this is your first Evolving Still product, I want to thank you for joining me on this journey. If this is not your first product I want to thank you for continuing to support me and am so grateful that these products have been beneficial to you. Striving to be an emotionally healthy person is not easy for most of us. In fact, it's one of the hardest things we've often done, so I am extremely thankful that you've trusted me along your journey.

Reflecting on this past year has made me realize just how important gratitude is, so it was only fitting that this year's journal would be Grate-ful: A Gratitude Journal. Gratitude is such an important practice and can seriously improve your life. It has been found to improve one's mood, self esteem, and even relationships. It has also been proved to reduce stress. Sometimes we get caught up in everything that is going on around us that we forget to be grateful for the important things. Truth be told, there are so many reasons to be grateful and the goal of this journal is to be intentional about acknowledging those reasons.

Inside you will find guided questions, quotes, and a few activities that promote gratitude. These tools are organized for Evolvers to use the journal weekly for about a year but there is no set order. You make the rules! You may notice a theme of the sun. The sun is often associated with new beginnings, power, healing and overall mood improvement. I hope this journal reminds you that no matter what is going on you can always be grateful for the sun.

Evolving still,

Eboni

What are the things that make you laugh?

What are the things that make you smile?

Who are the people in your village?

**WHAT IS BEING A FRIEND TO YOU?
MAKE A LIST OF ALL OF YOUR FRIENDS AND HOW LONG
YOU'VE BEEN FRIENDS WITH THEM.**

"Let gratitude be the pillow upon which you kneel to to say your nightly prayer. And let faith be the bridge you build to overcome evil and welcome good."

- Maya Angelou

What are your favorite things about you? What makes you unique?

Which life values are you grateful to have?

What mistakes are you grateful for making? How have you grown since then?

What is your greatest accomplishment to date?

"Thank you' is the best prayer that anyone could say. I say that one a lot. Thank you expresses extreme gratitude, humility, and understanding."

- Alice Walker

What is your greatest strength? How has this strength benefitted you recently?

WHAT WEAKNESS WERE YOU ABLE TO KEEP IN CHECK THIS WEEK?

What are your favorite life lessons?
Who do you think you would be without these lessons?

What 3 random things are you grateful for today?

> "This is a wonderful day.
> I've never seen this one before."
>
> — Maya Angelou

What is the best thing that has happened in your life in the last week?

WHAT ARE SOME THINGS YOU HAVE IMPROVED IN OVER THE LAST COUPLE OF YEARS?

What is your favorite thing about your life?

What is your favorite thing about the skin that you are in?

G̲r̲a̲t̲i̲t̲u̲d̲e̲ ̲A̲c̲t̲i̲v̲i̲t̲y̲

Eat your favorite meal today. Be intentional on enjoying and savoring the taste of this delicious dish.

Describe your favorite childhood memory/memories?

DESCRIBE YOUR FAVORITE PLACE IN THE WORLD.
HOW OLD WERE YOU
WHEN YOU FIRST EXPERIENCED THIS PLACE?

Describe your favorite food?
Why is this food so significant to you?

Describe your favorite drink? Why is this drink so significant to you?

"Gratitude is the closest thing to beauty manifested in an emotion."

- Mindy Kaling

What is your favorite purchase that you have made?

What is your favorite art form to experience? Describe the last time you experienced this?

What's one kind or thoughtful thing someone did for you recently?

What 6 random things are you grateful for today?

"There is always, always, always something to be thankful for."

- Unknown

What things are currently inspiring you?

In what ways have you grown in the past year?

What is your favorite family tradition?

What is your favorite personal tradition/ritual?

"Maybe being grateful means recognizing what you have for what it is. Appreciating small victories. Admiring the struggle it takes to simply be human."

- MEREDITH GREY, GREY'S ANATOMY

What do you love about this current season?
(Summer, Winter, Fall, Spring)

Which of the five senses are you most grateful for having?

List everyone you are grateful for knowing.

List everything that you can currently see right now that you are grateful for having.

Gratitude Activity

Tell someone that you are grateful for them and why.
They probably need to hear it.

In what ways are you able to help others?

What ways have others helped you?

Who is a teacher/mentor that you are grateful for having?

What 9 random things are you grateful for today?

"Gratitude opens the door, the power, the wisdom, and the creativity of the universe."

– Deepak Chopra

What book/tv show changed your life? What about it did you identify with?

What is a quote that you live by? Explain why?

What aspects of your city or neighborhood are you grateful for?

What is a skill that you are grateful for having?

"The roots of all goodness lie in the soil of appreciation for goodness."

-Dalai Lama

What was your last good laugh about?

WHAT ARE YOUR GUILTY PLEASURES?

At what times do you feel most confident?

What is the best compliment that you have ever received?

Gratitude Activity

Go out of your way to help someone out today. Whether it is calling a loved one and asking if they need anything or helping a stranger in the street. Whatever favor that you do will come back to you when you need it.

What do you love most about your friends?

What do you love most about your family?

What public figure are you grateful to have learned from? (Either living during your lifetime or before)

Which historical event positively impacted your life?

"You just want something else that someone else has, but that doesn't mean what you have isn't beautiful, because people always want what you have, and you always want what they have - no one is ever 100 percent."

- Rihanna

What things do you find comfort in?

WHAT IS A STRESSOR YOU ARE GRATEFUL TO HAVE PUT BEHIND YOU THIS YEAR?

In what ways have you grown in the past year?

What 12 random things are you grateful for today?

www.ingramcontent.com/pod-product-compliance
Lightning Source LLC
Chambersburg PA
CBHW042226160426
42811CB00117B/1069